GROUND ZERO DOGS

by Meish Goldish

Consultants:

Debra Tosch
Executive Director
National Disaster Search Dog Foundation
SearchDogFoundation.org

Ann Wichmann
Search and Rescue Dogs
of the United States
FEMA Canine Search Specialist (retired)

BEARPORT
PUBLISHING

New York, New York

WHITING PUBLIC LIBRARY
WHITING, IN 46394

Credits

Cover and Title Page, © F. Carter Smith; TOC, © Willam Baker Photography; 4, © Masatomo Kuriya/ Corbis; 5, © Spencer Platt/Getty Images; 6, © Justin Lane/The New York Times/Redux; 7, © Science Faction/SuperStock; 8, © Michael Rieger/FEMA News Photo; 9L, © Andrea Booher/FEMA News Photo; 9R, © AP Photo/Kathy Willens; 10, © AP Photo/Stephen Chernin; 11, © AP Photo/Paul Chiasson; 12, © Andrea Booher/FEMA News Photo; 13, © Willam Baker Photography; 14, © U.S. Navy/Preston Keres; 15, © Michael Rieger/FEMA News Photo; 16, © National Disaster Search Dog Foundation; 17, © National Disaster Search Dog Foundation; 18L, © Mpozi Mshale Tolbert/The Indianapolis Star; 18R, © American Veterinary Medical Association, with permission/Photo by: R. Scott Nolen; 19, © Michael Rieger/FEMA News Photo; 20L, © Stan Honda/AFP/Newscom; 20R, Courtesy of Suffolk County SPCA; 21, © AP Photo/Alan Diaz; 22, © Ryan Remiorz/AFP/Newscom; 23, © AP Photo/Alan Diaz; 24, © Ting-Li Wang/The New York Times/Redux; 25, © HOPE AACR/ Photo by Josiah Whitaker; 26, © Michael Rieger/FEMA News Photo; 27, © Tony Kurdzuk/Star Ledger/ Corbis; 28, © Michael Rieger/FEMA News Photo; 29TL, © Fotosearch; 29TR, © PhotoSpin; 29BL, © Fotosearch; 29BR, © Eric Isselée /Shutterstock.

Publisher: Kenn Goin
Editorial Director: Adam Siegel
Creative Director: Spencer Brinker
Design: Dawn Beard Creative
Photo Researcher: Picture Perfect Professionals, LLC

Library of Congress Cataloging-in-Publication Data

Goldish, Meish.
  Ground zero dogs / by Meish Goldish.
    p. cm. — (Dog heroes)
  Includes bibliographical references and index.
  ISBN 978-1-61772-576-0 (library binding) — ISBN 1-61772-576-5 (library binding)
 1. Rescue dogs—Juvenile literature. 2. September 11 Terrorist Attacks, 2001—Juvenile literature.
3. World Trade Center Site (New York, N.Y.)—Juvenile literature. I. Title.
  SF428.55.G65 2013
  636.7'0886—dc23

                            2012003341

Copyright © 2013 Bearport Publishing Company, Inc. All rights reserved. No part of this publication may be reproduced in whole or in part, stored in a retrieval system, or transmitted in any form or by any means, electronic, mechanical, photocopying, recording, or otherwise, without written permission from the publisher.

For more information, write to Bearport Publishing Company, Inc., 45 West 21st Street, Suite 3B, New York, New York 10010. Printed in the United States of America.

10 9 8 7 6 5 4 3 2 1

Table of Contents

A Deadly Attack

On the morning of September 11, 2001, **terrorists hijacked** two planes and crashed them into the twin towers of the World Trade Center in New York City. The first plane, carrying 92 people, hit the North Tower at 8:46 A.M. The second plane, carrying 65 people, flew into the South Tower at 9:03 A.M. The powerful explosions rocked the 110-story **skyscrapers**. Glass shattered and fires broke out on the upper floors where the planes struck.

Less than 20 minutes after the North Tower was hit, a second plane crashed into the South Tower.

Omar Rivera, a blind office worker, was on the 71st floor of the North Tower with his **guide dog**, Salty, when the first plane hit. Omar heard his coworkers screaming as they raced to the stairway to escape the burning building. With **chaos** all around, Salty grew nervous. Omar quickly told his dog to guide him down the stairs. Would Salty be able to lead his owner to safety?

Fuel from the planes caught fire after the crashes, causing the twin towers to burn.

The terrorists who flew the planes into the twin towers were members of a group called Al Qaeda (AHL KAY-duh), which was led by a man named Osama bin Laden.

Racing Against Time

Omar held on to Salty's **harness** as the two started down the smoky stairway. They walked on broken concrete and glass as firefighters hurried up the stairs, searching for survivors who were trapped in the building. Yet through all the confusion, Salty managed to remain calm. The brave dog moved forward at a steady pace, faithfully staying by his owner's side.

Omar and Salty, a yellow Labrador retriever

After an hour and fifteen minutes, Omar and Salty finally reached the ground floor. By then, the South Tower had **collapsed**. Omar and his dog quickly exited the North Tower and ran down the street. Minutes later, that building fell, too. Thanks to his brave dog, Omar had survived.

Damage from the fallen towers spread for many city blocks.

Another blind worker in the North Tower, Michael Hingson, was also saved by his guide dog, Roselle. The yellow Labrador retriever led him to safety from the 78th floor.

Dogs to the Rescue

After the towers fell, rescuers rushed in to search for survivors. The **Federal Emergency Management Agency** (FEMA) sent teams of workers, including about 80 **search-and-rescue dogs** and their **handlers**. The New York Police Department (NYPD) and other police organizations also provided dogs. Altogether, about 300 of the animals took part in the search-and-rescue effort. It was the largest **canine** rescue operation in U.S. history.

Giant mounds of sharp twisted metal and steel beams covered the area where the twin towers collapsed.

The work area where the twin towers once stood became known as Ground Zero. This term usually refers to the place where a bomb strikes the ground. As a result, it is the area of greatest destruction.

The search-and-rescue dogs that looked for victims were highly skilled. They had been trained and tested for work at disaster sites such as earthquakes and bombings. As a result, the dogs knew how to find people buried under **debris** by **detecting** their **scents**. They also knew how to climb ladders, walk along high beams, and crawl through dark, narrow tunnels during a search.

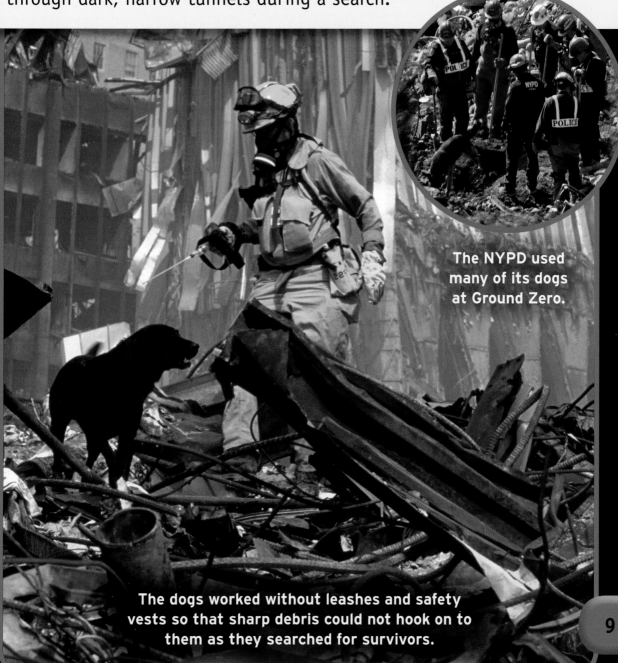

The NYPD used many of its dogs at Ground Zero.

The dogs worked without leashes and safety vests so that sharp debris could not hook on to them as they searched for survivors.

Searching for Survivors

When Canadian police officer James Symington heard about the attack in New York, he knew he had the perfect search-and-rescue dog to help out—Trakr. Thanks to his excellent sniffing skills, this seven-year-old German shepherd had found many missing people. James jumped into his car with his dog and drove for about 14 hours. They arrived at the disaster site early in the morning on September 12.

Police officer James Symington and his dog Trakr at Ground Zero

Trakr went to work immediately, sniffing large piles of **rubble** for any signs of life. At around 9:15 A.M., Trakr indicated a spot where he sensed a live person was buried. Firefighters dug in the debris. There they discovered Genelle Guzman-McMillan, an office worker from the North Tower who had been trapped for about 24 hours. Thanks to Trakr's sharp sense of smell, rescue workers were able to locate Genelle and dig her out of the debris.

Genelle Guzman-McMillan had tried to escape from the North Tower, but she had only reached the 13th floor when it fell. She is shown here recovering at a hospital after her rescue by Trakr.

Search-and-rescue dogs are trained to signal their handlers when they locate the scent of a live person. For example, FEMA dogs are taught to bark as a signal. Other dogs are also taught to sit down or dig at the spot.

A Special Nose

Trakr's discovery at Ground Zero was no accident. Dogs have an amazing sense of smell, which allows them to detect the scent of a human up to half a mile (.8 km) away. They can also smell a body buried as deep as 30 feet (9 m) in the ground.

Search-and-rescue dogs rely on their sense of smell to locate people who are hidden from view.

A dog's nose has up to 220 million **cells** for smelling, compared to only 5 million cells in a human's nose.

Search-and-rescue dogs are trained to recognize the scents of live people, dead bodies, or both. At Ground Zero, a German shepherd named Storm was unable to find any survivors. However, he located many bodies buried in the rubble. One time, he found seven victims lying under a large steel beam.

Storm and his handler, David Sanabria, worked for the NYPD.

On the Move

The handlers at Ground Zero hoped their canines would be able to find survivors before it was too late. Luckily, search-and-rescue dogs aren't just great sniffers. They can also move quickly. As a result, they can inspect a large area in a short amount of time.

Riley, a golden retriever, was strapped into a basket using his harness so that he could travel over a giant pit to get to his work area.

It can take 30 people an entire day to inspect a small fallen building. One search-and-rescue dog can check the same area in two hours or less.

Jenner was a Ground Zero dog that quickly searched the disaster site for victims. The black Labrador retriever carefully moved along twisted steel beams that lay on the ground. Sometimes he would disappear from sight and then suddenly pop up after discovering a body. Although Jenner didn't find any survivors, the bodies he found could at least be identified and returned to their families for burial.

Jenner and his handler, Ann Wichmann, were part of the FEMA rescue effort.

Following Orders

Search-and-rescue dogs move quickly through a disaster site, yet they don't work on their own. They learn to obey the **commands** of their handlers. For example, Abby, a Labrador retriever at Ground Zero, followed the orders of Debra Tosch. She called out commands such as "search," "**heel**," and "stay" as Abby quickly searched the area.

Debra watches Abby closely as her dog sniffs among the rubble.

If Abby moved along a beam too quickly, Debra ordered, "Wait." The dog stopped until her handler caught up. Abby also followed the hand signals that she had learned. They told her to move left, right, backward, or forward. With trucks, bulldozers, cranes, and other noisy equipment at Ground Zero, Debra had to **communicate** with Abby by hand as well as by voice.

Debra and Abby

Search-and-rescue dogs sometimes enter an area that is not safe for humans. Even though the dogs may be out of sight, the handlers must stay close enough so that they can hear the dogs if they bark to alert people that they have found someone.

17

WHITING PUBLIC L
ING, IN 46394

Danger on the Job

Even when following commands, the search-and-rescue dogs at Ground Zero sometimes got injured. On his second day at work, Kaiser, a German shepherd, badly sliced his front left paw. He probably cut it while walking on a piece of sharp steel. The dog wasn't upset, however. After **veterinarians** bandaged his paw, he happily returned to work.

Tony Zintsmaster, Kaiser's handler, praised his dog, saying, "He did what he was trained to do with a good attitude."

Kaiser relaxes after his injured paw was bandaged by vets.

Some Ground Zero dogs wore booties to protect their paws. Most, however, did not, because the feet coverings make it harder for the dogs to keep their balance while walking on difficult surfaces.

Another dog, a Belgian Malinois named Servus, accidentally fell into a pit at Ground Zero. It was full of dust and ash left by the burning remains of the fallen towers. The debris soon filled up the dog's nostrils, making it impossible for him to breathe. To save his life, Servus was rushed to a fire truck, where he was given **oxygen**. Police officers then brought him to an animal hospital. Veterinarians worked on the dog until he was breathing regularly again. By the next day, Servus was ready and eager to return to work.

At Ground Zero, smoky air filled with ash made it difficult to breathe—for people and dogs.

Handle with Care

The dogs at Ground Zero worked 12-hour **shifts** in areas filled with smoke, dust, and ash. If their health was ignored, the dogs could easily get sick. As a result, veterinarians at Ground Zero helped the handlers take good care of the brave canines. Besides tending to injuries, the vets checked and cleaned the dogs every day.

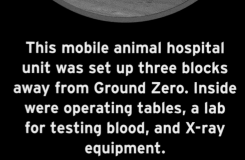

This mobile animal hospital unit was set up three blocks away from Ground Zero. Inside were operating tables, a lab for testing blood, and X-ray equipment.

Just nine hours after the attack, veterinarians arrived at Ground Zero to give medical care to the dogs.

More than 200 veterinarians worked at Ground Zero during the search-and-rescue effort.

After each shift, dogs like Jake, a Labrador retriever, were thoroughly examined. Vets tested Jake for **dehydration**. They checked his paws, eyes, and ears for injuries such as burns and cuts. They gave him a warm bath to remove dust and dirt from his fur, eyes, and nostrils. Jake and the other dogs even received **massages** to ease their aching muscles.

Jake and his handler, Mary Flood

Facing Sadness

Even with good medical care, many of the Ground Zero dogs suffered both physically and emotionally. They grew frustrated at not being able to find more survivors. Trakr's discovery of Genelle Guzman-McMillan turned out to be the very last rescue. After that, the dogs recovered only dead bodies.

A rescue worker and his dog rest after a long, hard work shift.

Handlers wanted to make sure the dogs didn't lose their desire to keep searching. As a result, some workers hid behind rubble so their dogs, eager to rescue someone, could "find" a live person. Dave Richards managed to cheer up his border collie, Cowboy, by giving him a squeaky toy to play with.

After the twin towers collapsed, only 20 people are known to have survived.

Cowboy searching for victims at Ground Zero

Easing the Pain

Just as workers cheered up dogs at Ground Zero, the dogs also cheered up workers. Max, a German shepherd, spent his work breaks with firefighters and police officers. They hugged and petted him. The contact brought **comfort** to the workers, who struggled with grief and stress on the job.

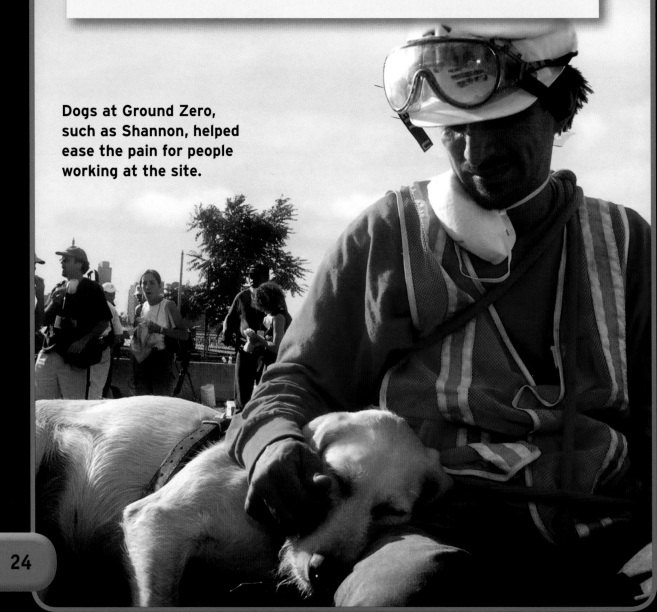

Dogs at Ground Zero, such as Shannon, helped ease the pain for people working at the site.

Therapy dogs were also brought to Ground Zero to cheer up workers. Tikva, a keeshond from Oregon, arrived with her handler, Cindy Ehlers. The dog walked around the site each day. She let workers pet her soft fur. It was a welcome change from the cold, hard steel they were used to handling on the job.

Therapy dogs visit places such as hospitals and nursing homes to cheer up people and make them feel more comfortable.

Workers at Ground Zero hugged Tikva, a soft, furry therapy dog.

Remembering Heroes

Most of the FEMA dogs worked at Ground Zero for five to ten days. After that, the tired dogs were sent home and replaced by a new team. The last FEMA dogs left the site around the beginning of October. Some NYPD police dogs, however, stayed at Ground Zero for up to eight months, recovering bodies and body parts. Today, more than ten years later, almost all of the dogs that took part in the search-and-rescue operation are no longer alive. However, they have not been forgotten.

A team of FEMA handlers and their dogs

Special ceremonies are held each year to honor the heroic canines. On the tenth anniversary of the attack, search-and-rescue dogs and their handlers held a **memorial** march at Liberty State Park in New Jersey, across the river from Ground Zero. The rescue teams had come from all over the country to recall with pride the Ground Zero dogs that had served their country so bravely.

Among the dogs honored at the memorial march was Sirius, a bomb-sniffing yellow Labrador retriever that was killed in the South Tower when it fell. He was the only dog to die in the World Trade Center attack.

The Liberty State Park memorial march in September 2011

Just the Facts

- Around 2,800 people died in the World Trade Center attack. They included 343 firefighters and 60 police officers who tried to rescue people in the towers before they fell.

- In addition to the planes that struck the World Trade Center, two other planes were also hijacked by Al Qaeda terrorists on September 11, 2001. The hijackers crashed one of the planes into the Pentagon in Arlington, Virginia, killing 184 people. The other plane crashed into a field near Shanksville, Pennsylvania, after passengers fought off the hijackers. Forty people were killed.

- In 2002, Salty and Roselle, the two guide dogs that led their blind owners to safety from the North Tower, received the Dickin Medal for their courage and loyalty. This highly valued British medal is awarded to animals that show extreme bravery in war.

- For years after the World Trade Center attack, veterinarians tracked the health of dogs that had worked at Ground Zero. They found that the canines stayed much healthier than human workers at the site. The animals did not develop the high rates of lung disease and cancer that people did.

Two rescue workers and their dogs taking a break at Ground Zero

GROUND ZERO DOGS

border collie

golden retriever

German shepherd

Labrador retriever

canine (KAY-nine) having to do with dogs

cells (SELZ) basic, very tiny parts of a person, animal, or plant

chaos (KAY-oss) total confusion

collapsed (kuh-LAPST) fell down or caved in

comfort (KUHM-furt) the feeling of being relaxed and free of pain or worries

commands (kuh-MANDZ) orders given by someone to do certain things

communicate (kuh-MYOO-nuh-kayt) to share information or ideas

debris (duh-BREE) the scattered pieces of something that has been destroyed

dehydration (*dee*-hye-DRAY-shuhn) a lack of water in one's body

detecting (di-TEKT-ing) noticing or discovering something

Federal Emergency Management Agency (FED-ur-uhl i-MUR-juhn-see MAN-ihj-muhnt AY-juhn-see) a U.S. government organization that helps communities prepare for and recover from natural and human-made disasters

guide dog (GIDE DAWG) a dog that is trained to lead a blind person from place to place

handlers (HAND-lurz) people who train and work with animals

harness (HAR-niss) a device attached to an animal that allows people to hold on to the animal

heel (HEEL) when a dog walks on the left side of a person

hijacked (HYE-jakt) took control of an airplane or other vehicle by force

massages (muh-SAHZH-uhz) body rubs that relax the muscles

memorial (muh-MOR-ee-uhl) something that is meant to help people remember a person or an event

oxygen (OK-suh-juhn) a colorless gas that is found in the air and water, and that animals and people need to breathe

rubble (RUHB-uhl) pieces of broken concrete, bricks, and other building material

scents (SENTS) smells or odors

search-and-rescue dogs (SURCH-AND-RES-kyoo DAWGZ) dogs that look for lost people or survivors after a disaster, such as an earthquake

shifts (SHIFTS) set periods of time when people or animals work

skyscrapers (SKYE-*skray*-purz) very tall buildings

terrorists (TER-ur-ists) people who use violence and threats to achieve their goal

veterinarians (*vet*-ur-uh-NAIR-ee-uhnz) doctors who treat sick or injured animals

Bibliography

Bauer, Nona Kilgore. *Dog Heroes of September 11th: A Tribute to America's Search and Rescue Dogs.* Freehold, NJ: Kennel Club Books (2011).

Dumas, Charlotte. *Retrieved.* Los Angeles: The Ice Plant (2011).

Guzman-McMillan, Genelle, with William Croyle. *Angel in the Rubble: The Miraculous Rescue of 9/11's Last Survivor.* New York: Howard Books (2011).

Jackson, Donna M. *Hero Dogs: Courageous Canines in Action.* New York: Little, Brown and Company (2003).

McCarthy, Mick, and Patricia Ahern. *In Search of the Missing: Working with Search and Rescue Dogs.* Cork, Ireland: Mercier Press (2011).

Read More

McDaniel, Melissa. *Disaster Search Dogs (Dog Heroes).* New York: Bearport (2005).

Miller, Marie-Therese. *Search and Rescue Dogs.* New York: Chelsea Clubhouse (2007).

Osborne, Mary Pope, and Natalie Pope Boyce. *Dog Heroes.* New York: Random House (2011).

Learn More Online

Visit these Web sites to learn more about search-and-rescue dogs:

disasterdog.org

fema.gov/emergency/usr/canine.shtm

sardogsus.org

searchdogfoundation.org/98/html/1-deployments/1-2_wtc.html

zoenature.org/2011/09/meet-one-of-the-dog-teams

Index

About the Author

Meish Goldish has written more than 200 books for children. His book *Heart-Stopping Roller Coasters* was a Children's Choices Selection in 2011. He lives in Brooklyn, New York, not far from Ground Zero.

WHITING PUBLIC LIBRARY
WHITING, IN 46394